We Look Back and Sing!

A History of the Spirituals

Willie Mae Jordan

Illustrations by Robert Hall

Archway Publishing books may be ordered through booksellers or by contacting:

Archway Publishing
1663 Liberty Drive
Bloomington, IN 47403
www.archwaypublishing.com
1-(888)-242-5904

Because of the dynamic nature of the Internet, any web addresses or links contained in
this book may have changed since publication and may no longer be valid. The views
expressed in this work are solely those of the author and do not necessarily reflect the
views of the publisher, and the publisher hereby disclaims any responsibility for them.

Any people depicted in stock imagery provided by Thinkstock are models,
and such images are being used for illustrative purposes only.

Certain stock imagery © Thinkstock.

ISBN: 978-1-4808-0395-4 (sc)
ISBN: 978-1-4808-0394-7 (e)

Printed in the United States of America

Archway Publishing rev. date: 2/3/2015

FOREWORD

From the dismal bowels of ships bound on a wretched journey, guttural wails ascended from hostages held below its decks. The haunting sounds of iron manacles and shackled limbs lingered beyond splintered floors, past the breaking of salt water waves, as their cries called out to the highest heavens.

In the abyss of even the darkest fleets, sorrowful moans were given a voice of hope in form of a song. Tormented screams found comfort in the uncomplicated soothing melodies.

The sound erupted from the land where labor was forced. Songs from the walls of shacks were filled with anguish, fatigue, and dreams of freedom, as it traveled through woods that sheltered secretive trails, and uncharted paths. Hums, lyrics, and rhythms spread across the terrain from musical Griots. They sang the songs of better days.

During the darkest nights and hottest days, hope and the courage to live touched souls forever. It was, and is, music that is ordained, housed inside the temple of mankind, and its name is Spiritual.

The Spiritual continues to transform along its journey. It is often the first musical sound heard in the African American experience. It's the creative gift, and offering from The Most High, as a direct line stored in the collective memories of souls. And, it is the extension connecting the past, the present, and future.

To paraphrase Willie Mae Jordan, the author... When you know your ancestry, the history that pours from within, ignites you with the ability, forethought, and willingness to stand as an individual determined and destined to make the world.

W.B. Gunter

INTRODUCTION

The inspiration for this book begins with the moans and grunts of the unsung melody of pain in the belly of a slave ship circa 1619. One can only imagine the horrific torture our African ancestors endured as a result of this experience, which took a lot of agonizing time to cross the ocean from continent to continent. Somehow, the slaves endured.

This endurance inspired what initially was called "the Negro spiritual." These songs of lasting beauty accompanied the slaves' work. The use of the natural instruments, such as the clapping of the hands and the tapping of the feet, accompanied their voices. The great African-American composer, Mr. Edward Boatner, describes the spiritual as "the original folk music of America."

This country is not able to claim the opera, symphony, art song or any other European form of music. We award the spiritual as being the first "American music."

As an undergraduate alumnus of Virginia State and graduate alumnus of Eastern Michigan University, I am grateful for the formal training that prepared me to research this book.

As an alumnus of the American Institute of Musical Studies in Graz, Styria, Austria, I was able to perform publicly, singing spirituals, and I really began to appreciate this form as universal.

These many experiences, as performer and educator, inspired me to create "Tiny Tunes," my prized, trademarked curriculum for children, which reveals the history and songs of the slaves' spirituals.

My wish is that this book will help preserve the messages of songs in code, call and response, Bible stories and hymns. Passing down these messages in original form to our children will allow the spirituals to prevail for the duration of humanity.

I am not compelled to use any musical notations in this work. The slaves' limited knowledge of written music resulted in creation of memorable melodies and lyrics that have flowed from generation to generation.

*Our ancestors moaned and
grunted in the belly of the ship.*

CHAPTER I

The story of the spirituals began many years ago. People who look like you and me were taken away from their families and from their continent Africa. Mothers were separated from fathers. Sisters and brothers were separated. This was called the slave trade, which began many years ago, even before my great-grandparents were born.

All slaves were placed in the belly of the ship, tied in chains on the neck, hands, legs and feet. The sounds of the slaves are described as moans and grunts and cries. The pain of separation from family and other loved ones made them very, very sad.

The slaves had not forgotten the music and beats of their African homeland. When they landed on American soil, moans and grunts became melody and took on words like these:

"Sometimes I feel like a motherless child; sometimes I feel like a motherless child; sometimes I feel like a motherless child a long ways from home, a long ways from home.

"Sometimes I feel like I'm almost gone; sometimes I feel like I'm almost gone; sometimes I feel like I'm almost gone a long ways from home, a long ways from home."

The spirituals are code songs.

CHAPTER II

The slaves began to grow in great numbers on the plantations in America. In the South, like our states of North Carolina and Virginia, the owners of the slaves made them work very hard in the harvest of the fields. Our ancestors, the slaves, created and made up songs, called "the spirituals," to sing as they worked.

These very beautiful songs also helped the slaves to keep secrets from their masters or owners. The songs became known as "code songs."

The secret message would tell the slaves about a runaway trip to freedom. A song such as "Get on Board Little Children" would tell slaves about a kind of train leaving the plantation. They did not have to pay money to travel this train. It was called the "Underground Railroad."

Of course, there was no such thing as an underground railroad or a train to travel on. Instead, there were secret roads to travel, and safe houses where slaves could hide as they escaped.

A very strong, courageous woman, Harriet Tubman, led this so-called "Underground Railroad" to free the slaves. Known as the black Moses, she freed her family members and hundreds of other slaves journeying this railroad.

The spiritual "Go Down Moses" sent the message to America to "let my people go:"

"Go down Moses, way down in Egypt land. Tell ol' Pharaoh, let my people go."

Another secret message about escaping to freedom went like this: "Swing low, sweet chariot, comin' for to carry me home. Swing low, sweet chariot, comin' for to carry me home."

Sometimes, the slaves had to cross water as they escaped, as in: "Wade in the water; wade in the water, children; wade in the water. God's a-gonna trouble the water."

A final message before taking off to freedom might be: "Steal away, steal away, steal away home. I ain't got long to stay here."

The spirituals are call and response.

CHAPTER III

There were a few times that slaves were allowed to play games, celebrate holidays, and come together as groups to sing.

Sometimes, there would be a slave, male or female, who had a beautiful voice. This person would be the leader to sing the lead, or call. The others in the group would sing an answer, or response.

"Go Down Moses" is also an example of this call and response style:

Call: When Israel was in Egypt's land,
Response: Let my people go.
Call: Oppressed so hard they could not stand,
Response: Let my people go. Go down Moses, way down in Egypt's land. Tell ol' Pharaoh, let my people go.
Call: Thus sayeth the Lord, bold Moses said,
Response: Let my people go.
Call: If not, I'll smite your first-born dead,
Response: Let my people go. Go down Moses. Go down Moses. Go down Moses. Let my people go.

Another call and response spiritual is "Swing Low, Sweet Chariot."

Call: I'm sometimes up and sometimes down.
Response: Comin' for to carry me home.
Call: But still my soul is heavenly bound.
Response: Comin' for to carry me home. Swing low, sweet chariot, comin' for to carry me home. Swing low, sweet chariot, comin' for to carry me home.
Call: If you get there before I do,
Response: Comin' for to carry me home.
Call: Tell all my friends I'm a- comin', too.
Response: Comin' for to carry me home.

The call is a different idea, but the repeated response is the same and makes the idea strong.

The spiritual "Wade in the Water" has the same kind of call and response. The spiritual is as follows:

Call: See that band all dressed in red.
Response: God's a-gonna trouble the water.

Call: Looks like the band that Moses led.

Response: God's a-gonna trouble the water. Wade in the water; wade in the water, children. Wade in the water. God's a-gonna trouble the water.

Call: See that band all dressed in white.

Response: God's a-gonna trouble the water.

Call: It looks like the band of Israelites.

Response: God's a-gonna trouble the water. Wade in the water; wade in the water, children; wade in the water. God's a-gonna trouble the water.

The spirituals are Bible stories.

CHAPTER IV

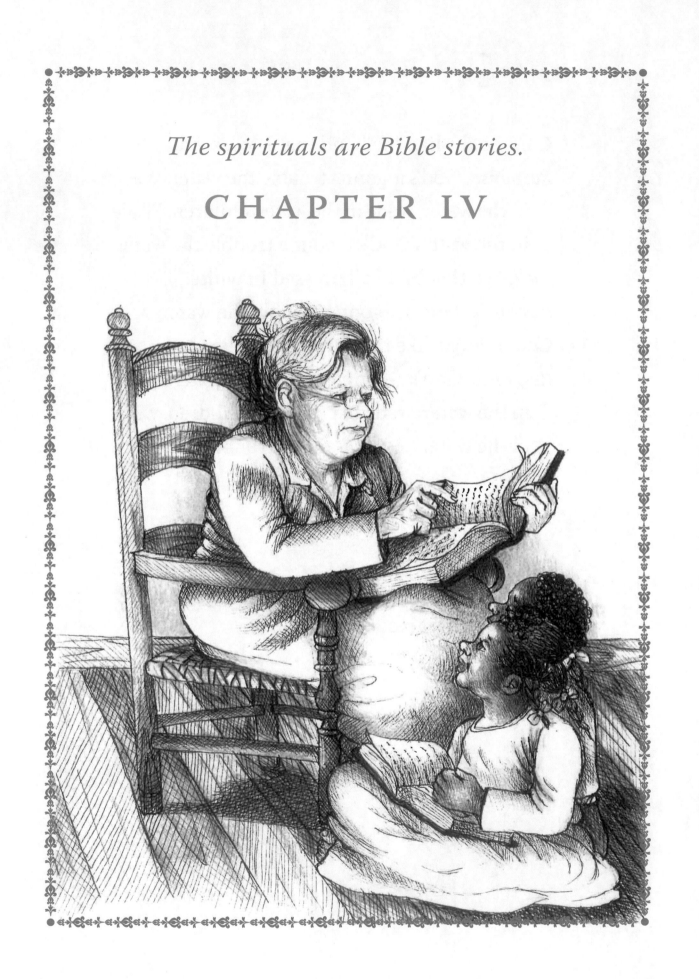

Slaves were often taught by the mistress, the wife of their owner and master. Their textbook was the Bible. This teaching was done in secret because slaves were not allowed to read. A favorite story of the slaves was of the ancient Hebrew leader, Moses.

Many years ago, the Moses in the Bible freed the Israelites, or Hebrew children, as they were called. Our slave ancestors imagined themselves being led to freedom by "the black Moses," Harriet Tubman.

The spiritual "Go Down Moses" referred to Mrs. Tubman, who helped free the American slave children.

The prophet Ezekiel was another Bible story favorite of our ancestors. The slaves loved characters with visions. Visions are dreams. This story is from the Old Testament Book of Ezekiel, Chapter 1, Verse 6. In Ezekiel's vision, he saw the wheels of chariots leading to heaven.

The slaves had visions of these wheels taking them to a better place, inspiring the spiritual:

"Ezekiel saw the wheel, way up in the middle of

the air. Ezekiel saw the wheel, way up in the middle of the air.

"The big wheel run by faith. And the little wheel run by the grace of God. Ezekiel saw the wheel, way in the middle of the air."

The spiritual "Balm in Gilead" is taken from the Old Testament's Jeremiah, Chapter 8, Verse 22. The Civil Rights leader, Dr. Martin Luther King Jr., talked about this spiritual in a speech at the AME African Methodist Episcopal Conference in 1964 in Cincinnati, Ohio. Dr. King addressed the question that the prophet Jeremiah pondered, which is why the unjust people prospered and the just people suffered or did not do well.

Jeremiah asked the question, "Is There a Balm in Gilead?" He meant to say, "can the good people be healed and live well?"

Dr. King said, centuries later, that our ancestors looked back and straightened that question mark and proclaimed, "There Is a Balm in Gilead to make the wounded whole!"

The spirituals are hymns.

CHAPTER V

A good number of slaves held church in what was secretly called the "bush arbor." A group of slaves would gather in the woods or near a waterfront away from their world of endless work.

Spirituals were created in the hymn style of singing. For this type of spiritual there are three or more verses sung to the same melody. The spiritual, "Lord, I Want to Be a Christian," is a beautiful example:

Verse 1: "Lord, I want to be a Christian in-a-my heart, in-a-my heart. Lord, I want to be a Christian in-a-my heart, in-a-my heart. In-a-my heart, in-a-my heart; Lord, I want to be a Christian in-a-my heart.

Verse 2: "Lord, I want to be like Jesus, in-a-my heart, in-a-my heart. Lord, I want to be like Jesus, in-a-my heart, in-a-my heart. In-a-my heart, in-a-my heart; Lord, I want to be like Jesus in-a-my heart.

Verse 3: "Lord, I want to be more loving in-a-my heart, in-a-my heart. Lord, I want to be more loving, in-a-my heart, in-a-my heart. In-a-my heart, in-a-my heart; Lord, I want to be more loving in-a-my heart.

Verse 4: "Lord, I don't want to be like Judas in-a-my heart, in-a-my heart. Lord, I don't want to be like Judas in-a-my heart, in-a-my heart. In-a-my heart, in-a-my heart; Lord, I don't want to be like Judas in-a-my heart."

When the slaves were on their journey to freedom, there were people along the way who supported their cause. Free Negroes, Whites, and Native Americans opened the doors to their homes to give the slaves a resting place.

The presence of a lighted candle in the window let the slaves know that a safe place was available to stay.

The spiritual, "This Little Light of Mine," told the story:

Verse 1: "This little light of mine, I'm gonna let it shine. This little light of mine, I'm gonna let it shine. This little light of mine, I'm gonna let it shine, let it shine, let it shine, let it shine.

Verse 2: "All through the night, I'm gonna let it shine. All through the night, I'm gonna let it shine. All through the night, I'm gonna let it shine, let it shine, let it shine, let it shine.

Verse 3: "Everywhere I go, I'm gonna let it shine. Everywhere I go, I'm gonna let it shine. Everywhere I go, I'm gonna let it shine, let it shine, let it shine, let it shine."

Today, our light still shines in the windows of our lives.

THE END

ACKNOWLEDGEMENTS

This author is very pleased to thank the following persons for helping me to make this body of work a reality; Wanda (W.B.) Gunter, body of work coordinator; Carrie G. Brock, copy editor; William H. Brock III, computer analyst; Sharon Brown, manuscript typist/editor, proofreader; Martha Spencer, manuscript typist; Richard C. Griffin III, supervising manager; Linda Wellons, biographer, proofreader; Cheryl Hanes, biographer; Robert Hall, illustrator; Don Hill, spiritual interpreter; Ken Wilson, portrait artist; La Volta Restaurant, downtown, Raleigh, NC., corporate supporters; Chick-Fil-A, downtown, Raleigh, NC., corporate sponsorship; Paul Bryant, private donor; The Carolinian Newspaper, Raleigh, NC., The Anchor News Newspaper, Waco, TX.;

Martin Street Baptist Church Book Club, Raleigh, NC., Authors' Recognition.

Special thanks goes to all of my family, the teachers, and other individuals, too numerous to name, for your endless support. This author is also very thankful to the Archway Publishing team for their splendid job of making this body of work a reality; William Curry, consultant; Adriane Pontecorvo, book preproduction; Emma Gliessman, book production; and Rebecca Hogue, marketing.

Printed in the United States
by Baker & Taylor Publisher Services